OCEAN OF DREAMS AND THOUGHTS

HARNOOR KAUR

Contents

Preface

This book contains a set of poems which have been written with immense love. Sometimes life teaches you to be strong despite of all the hatred and hurt you are getting. But deep inside you still felt that hurt inside you but you choose to move with a smile. Many times in my life I have moved on from contionous hurt that I get from people not because I didn't wanted to get hurt but it was just that I wanted peace in my life. It's rightly said that " Do not let the behavior of other's destroy your inner peace" So be happy and don't forget to love yourself!

Acknowledgements

I would like to thank all the people who supported me. Especially my parents who have been my guiding force and my great inspiration. I would also like to thank my friends who were with me at every stage of life and made me believed that i can do this. I also want to thank my brother who has been my great support. My teacher's who guided me at every step. I also want to thank my dog Rocky, people may find it weird but without speaking a word he made me realize the importance of self love.

I also shall like to thank Notion Press for believing in me. I am very thankful for the support that you provided. I apologize if I missed someone but I am truly grateful to each and everyone who was there with me at every moment.

And especially thank you to those who criticized me or left me because your critism and exit made me stronger. And last but not least thank you to the readers for choosing this book.

Prologue

1. EXISTENCE

Soo many people come on this Earth
With a purpose in their eyes
But deep inside
This all is a lie
The alarm goes off at 6:00AM
Like everyday
Making you get up from bed
So that you can go to work for the job you hate
And curse your fate
Always waiting for the day
When they can start to live
But the day they start to live is the day
They have an end
This is what I'm scared of
Soon I'll become like them
Only walking with the crowd
Because my dreams have been suppressed
Some by my family and some by society
And one day I'll look back
At all the opportunities I missed
And realize I never truly lived
All I did was just exist!

2. WORLD OF MY DREAMS

Like all the teenage girls

I don't dream to be in a fairyland

I don't want to be in a world of fairytale just like Rapunzel

I just want to peace in my life

and a pinch of freedom

Freedom to speak , freedom to live

Freedom to be what I wanna be

Freedom from all the comments of people

Freedom to be judged from society

This is what all I want

I hope I'm not asking much

' Cause I'm tired of this all

I'm tired of the continuous nagging

and of repeatedly criticism

So let me be the way I want to be

This is how my world of dream is

It is nothing like the world of fairytales but

it is another peaceful- happy life !

3. TIME

The minute hand and the second hand never stops
That's why the movie of life never flops
Time is something that moves on
And does not wait for someone mourns
People come and go
But time never stops
It is precious as gold and flows like water
It passes by like wind
Making think every mind its importance
Why we cry after wasting it
And not spend it before ruining it
Time is something to be used wisely
Not to be wasted that nicely
We are given numbered hours and minutes
From the never - ending journey of time
And nobody knows when this relay race
Will end for us for someone else to takeover
So why not make the best out of what we're left with
Maybe some days , some hours or some minutes!

4. LOVE

Love: a word full of emotions
A solution to all the problems
But it will hurt you sooner or later
Today or Tomorrow
This year or next year
Love will surely tear you part
And will take some people apart
But then this is what life is
People leave and that's okay
Move on and except it
But is it that easy?
To leave someone you love
To forget someone you love
Indeed, it is difficult
If you will go through it you will get to know
It's difficult to deal with it
To see that person with someone else is
An arduous situation
This is not so happy relationship
To be in love with someone who is unsure
About its own situationship
So stop looking for love
It will find a way on its own
If it is meant to be it will be truly yours !

5. CHANGE IN SEASONS

People change like seasons
Sometimes it's summer
Then it's winter
Other time it's rainy
And next is autumn
The change in people hurt us
But change in seasons doesn't
But why do they change?
It's a question that is never answered
If you find it then let me know
Maybe they find someone new
A better version of a few
So stop crying on their exist
And be happy on the entrance of new
Stop worrying about useless relations
And start paying attention towards some lovable relations
Love yourself before you love someone else
As self love is always the best !

6. MY SHINING STAR

An angel lives among me
Which is sent by God from above
Her smile is something I love
Her sadness is something that I hate
She sacrificed alot for me and she is still doing
I can't thank her enough for all the things she do's
Ur my best frnd , Ur my guide
Ur my sunshine , Ur my star
Thank you for making our house
A little more like a home
Ur a garden, a garden of heart
You planted all the good things that gave my life its start
You turned me to sunshine and encouraged me too dream
Fostering and nurturing
The seeds of self- esteem
It hurts to see people leaving ,But then I
Remember your face
My forever partner who's gonna stay wid me always
And even though I hardly say it , I love you quite alot
Ur not just my mother but my shining bright star

7. SEVEN OLD YEAR SELF

If I met my seven year old self today
Will I let her live or warn her about the future
What would I say?
Will I caution her about the future
Of the bad things yet to come ?
Or would I leave her to be naive
To keep having fun?
Because my seven year old self
Believed in perfect world
World of best people and best things
Would she recognize herself
When she will look into my eyes
Will she recognize the hurt that changed me?
Even though I've learnt soo much more
And ten years have passed since then
I would give everything I have
To view my life through her eyes again
And live the life of seven old year over again!

8. F.R.I.E.N.D.S

F.R.I.E.N.D.S is not just a seven letter word
But a word full of emotions
They are sunshine to my sun
And light to my stars
They are cream to my cupcake
And cherry to my cake
They are chalk to my board
And fuel to my car
I feel like I'm the moon
And they are my stars
I'm just a body , they act like my food
They make me feel happy in every mood
They are my umbrella in my rain
Behind the hidden smile they find my pain
They are my life jacket
And nitrogen to my chips packet
I want them to stay forever with me
Because there is no one like them
It isn't the red ribbon that binds us together
The root that unifies us does not derive
From a tree on the wall
All we can say is this bond knows no genetics!

9. LIFE OF TEENAGERS

The life of teenagers is never easy
It's not that good
As you think it to be
For once if you enter their world
You will know their good
The critism they face , the bullying they face
And soo many things they need to prove in their case
It's hard being a teenager
You really don't know what to do
You're not a child not yet an adult
You wish you never grew
Teenage life is nothing but more pressure everyday
To be even better
Than the year just gone through
We learn from our mistakes
From the wrong turns we take
From the fake friends we make
And from the times we almost break
It's hard be a teenager but still we are going through that phase
And fighting that tough case !

10. TOM AND JERRY

A relation pure like gold
Is the relation of brother and sister
Together they dream
Together they fight
Life's most important lessons
To each other they teach
Together they laugh
Together they cry
But they remain with each other like Tom stays with Jerry
Together they succeed
Together they fail
Out of all life's problem
Each other they bail
They are like the life jackets to each other
One is imperfect without the other
Together as friends they face the world
Joy or laughter or tear or strife
Holding hands Together they dance
Through the phase of life
This is the only bond that is deeply seeded inside the pot of heart !

11. WHY SHE CHANGED?

If you knew her
You'd know words feel her up
The sudden change in people's behavior
Made her change herself
Giving hopes to someone and then leaving
Is what people actually do
What happened I have no clue
Crying at night And facing the trauma
Sleeping all day just to skip this melodrama
She's now afraid to love someone
To hold someone's hand
To care for someone else
To be someone's something
She's terrified to give her everything as she did last time
She realized that she was no one to them
Who she considered her gems
She still cries at night
But walks with a smile in a day
She realized it soon you can't be the only one fighting may be relationship or friendship
Because we can't be the only one struggling in this hardship !

12. IMPRINT

I should have made you mine
and our relation could have been fine like a wine
My love for you is never getting less
Even if our bond becomes a mess
Seeing you with someone else
Will eventually make me sad
So if I shout on you don't be mad
I wish you would have chosen me
And not acted so mean
In these days ,you have changed is what I have seen
People think it is love of teen
But it is something that cannot be erased from the state of my heart
Because it is imprinted on my soul!

13. SELF LOVE

A bright sunny day
is ahead of you
New opportunities are
waiting for you
Stop worrying about
others and start loving yourself
As self love is the best love
So start caring for yourself
than caring for others
Because at the end people don't appreciate others
Instead of wasting your love on shifty people
Love yourself like love of mother
Trust yourself like no other
Pay attention to your own health
and make yourself better than others
Stop worrying about people's comments
and remember that you're beautiful
Don't be anxious about past and live the movement
People may comment on you
But keep in mind there's someone out who adores you!

14. PARENTS AND THEIR PERSEPECTIVE

Parents are always right;

No doubt about that

and children are always wrong

that's something to doubt upon

Parents are right even if they are against the wishes of a child

And children are always wrong even if they abide by their parents

You are arguing with me that means you are disrespecting me this is
what parents feel

If we children put our point that is a bad deed

You are going on wrong side

It's because of your phone

You are scoring less marks

That's a minus point of a phone

But it is something to understand

That phone is not always the cause

Sometimes it's lack of some skill or concentration or some mental
stress

That leads to this mislead

I am not saying that parents are unfair

But I'm not even saying that we children are always sinful!

15. TEACHINGS OF LIFE

• 15 •

Life taught me alot
To live without someone
To not trust blindly
To stop asking people's opinion
Is what I learned latter
I hope I knew it before
If I had I would have Not been that hurt
But this is how life goes on
It is a experience with mixed emotions
A bit of sadness and a pinch of happiness
Worrying about things only gives anxiety
It is nothing but a cause that leads to the end of a happy life
Rather than thinking about it
Move on or work upon it
Because this is the only solution to this prevailing problem!

16. FRENEMY

There are so many degrees in the world
That can be done by people
But they want to play blame game
And make excuses that are so lame
The people who supported them in every stage of life
They back stabbed them with a knife
Whatever you do for them that is not gruff for them
So stop making effort for them
Playing games is not what friendship is about
But if you want to play games then I will show you how we do it
I'd rather sweat a bucket to search out peace
Than spilling blood fighting demons around me
God gave me common sense to understand so that I can walk away
There's more you will never now
What goes on behind a wall
In my mistake you have been proud
Like you were selfish bird
I got to see your real view
At this point our friendship ends
I was foolish to believe in you
You were just a frenemy!

17. A TOUGH DECISION

A tough decision
I had to make
I am happy
That I had to fake
I'm okay without you
Was just a beautiful lie
I'm yours and you're mine was another hopeless lie
You caught me in your oily words and made me fall in love
The love you showed me that day made me fall for you tighter
But who knew
That love will soon turn out to be my worst nightmare
I loved you more than I loved myself
But at the end what I got was a hopeless, lonely self!

18. RESTRICTIONS ON GIRLS

People judge us at every moment

At every pace

They comment on us at every place

You are skinny , eat more

You are fat , eat less

Wear your clothes properly

Or else stay back at home

So many restrictions on girls

Can you please tell me why?

We are too human being

Don't do this , Don't go there

That's all we hear

Why are all restrictions for us ?

Why are boys not restricted?

People tend to shout at girls

Even when she is not at fault

Why we have to bear the consequences

Whether we have done it or not

So please don't restrict us

Let we be a free bird

And Don't make our life blurred

We also have a life to live, so let us live

Let them bloom, let them all shine like a beautiful moon!

19. COURT OF LIFE

In the court of life

In standing in solitude

Allegation is what I'm facing

Criticism is something we are now familiar with

But people are unfamiliar with the damage it does

But do they care?

Not really,I know

They hate me because they can't be me

They disrespect me because they don't respect themselves

They talk behind my back

And act like good in front

They use the makeup of MAC

And say that they are natural

Oh! Please remove your mask

A mask : of goodness, of truthfulness, of loyalty and love

Be real, Be you

Instead of acting like others

You hate me say it

You love me say it

But just don't fake it

I'm perfect ,I admit it, But are you perfect?

But actually no one is

So think before you comment on me

Because at the end you're also a double faced being!

20. CLOUDS

Clouds have appeared
And they cannot be disappeared
Problems have always been with me
Like Tom stays with Jerry
Clouds are now very dark and full of rain
They are soon going to burst and give plenty of rain
Same way I'm full of tears and ready to overflow
'Cause there is no other way out
Clouds have to burst and tears have to fell down
But remember there's always sunshine after the thunderstorm
Sun has to come
And Problems have to go
Life will be difficult but not always it will be that hard
Difficulties are a integral part of life
Without it you cannot identify your own real self
Without it you cannot make out your real ones
It's hard and not that easy
But this how life works
You have to walk down through storm to witness the bright colorful
rainbow !

WHEN LIFE GIVES YOU HUNDRED REASONS TO BREAK DOWN AND CRY,

SHOW LIFE THAT YOU HAVE MILLION REASONS TO SMILE AND LAUGH.

STAY STRONG!